# PARROT ABC's

By Luanne Shear

For my Luke and my flock

# Aa

A is for African grey parrot.

# B b

B is for Blue-and-Gold macaw.

# Cc

C is for Cockatiel.

# Dd

D is for Dusky-headed conure.

# Ee

E is for Eclectus parrot.

# Ff

F is for Fig parrot.

# Gg

G is for Galah cockatoo.

# Hh

H is for Hawk-headed parrot.

# Ii

I is for Indian ringneck parakeet.

# Jj

J is for Jardine parrot.

# Kk

K is for Kakapo parrot.

# Ll

L is for Lovebird.

# Mm

M is for Meyer's parrot.

# Nn

N is for Nanday conure.

O is for Orange-winged amazon.

# P p

P is for Pionus parrot.

# Qq

Q is for Quaker parakeet.

# Rr

R is for Rosy bourke parakeet.

S s

S is for Senegal parrot.

# T t

T is for Turquoise parrot.

# U u

U is for Umbrella cockatoo.

V is for Violet-necked lory.

# Ww

W is for White-fronted amazon.

X is for Mexican red-headed amazon.

Y is for Yellow-collared macaw.

# Zz

Z is for Cuban ama<u>z</u>on.

# Zz

Z is for Cuban ama<u>z</u>on.